Chaos: Volume 1

A Journal of Being Human

Scott Burton

To connect with the author, find him on Instagram: **@ks.bleeds.ink**

Or

www.ScottBurtonAuthor.com

Printed in the United States of America

First Edition

ISBN (Paperback): 978-1-967979-00-4

ISBN (eBook): 978-1-967979-01-1

Also by Scott Burton

Forever is Tomorrow
(Second Edition, 2022)

Chaos: Volume 2 – *A Study of Shadows*
Chaos: Volume 3 – *The Weight of a Memory*
Chaos: Volume 4 – *A Study of Truths Unspoken*
Chaos: Volume 5 – *A Study of Distance*
Chaos: Volume 6 – *The Anatomy of Doubt*
Chaos: Volume 7 – *A Map of What Remains*
Chaos: Volume 8 – *A Theory of Falling*
Chaos: Volume 9 – *A Tether to Tomorrow*
Chaos: Volume 10 – *A Testament to the Quiet*

Dedication

For everyone who has ever felt too much, too long, too deep.

These pages are for the ones who carry silence like weight, who feel everything and wonder if it's too much, too late, or too often.

They are fragments of a shared world—the emotional landscapes we walk through quietly, the questions we carry without answers, and the moments that remind us we're never as alone as we fear.

This is for you. For us. For the becoming.

*The world speaks in whispers, and sometimes we
are the ones listening loudest.*

Preface

Before we knew how to name the ache, we felt it.

This is a beginning, in the loosest sense.
Not a start—but a noticing.

A recognition of what it means to exist.
To be seen.
To want more than what's given but not know
how to ask for it.

There's no grand discovery here.
Only fragments. Glimpses.
A voice testing the shape of truth in a world that
moves too fast to hear it.

Maybe being human isn't about finding answers.
Maybe it's just learning how to hold what
trembles—and not let go.

Part I: The Horizon That Doesn't Wait

There is no arrival. Only the act of becoming.

Scott Burton

Chapter 1: The Weight of Silence

I used to speak in whispers—glances that begged for understanding, sentences half-formed and swallowed. But silence has a weight to it, and over time, it became too heavy to carry between us.

It settled in the pauses, in the hesitation between "I'm fine" and what I really wanted to say. I often wonder if you knew—if you ever noticed the things I didn't say, the ache behind quiet eyes.

Or maybe you were waiting too. Caught in your own silence. Drowning in your own unspoken truths.

Somewhere between us, in all the places words should have lived, something faded. And now I walk through echoes—replaying old conversations, reaching for pieces of us I lost between the cracks.

Chapter 2: Clipped Wings

Five stories up, I watched the world burn.

Children ran toward lifeless bodies they once called Mother. Smoke rose like fragile prayers. I stared down at the chaos and wondered who we expected to save us.

Who was ever going to teach us to fly?

I used to believe in the system. I really did. But belief in something that never believed in you is a kind of self-betrayal.

And now? I just want wings that work. Wings that haven't been clipped for thinking differently, for feeling too deeply.

But I never learned to fly on broken wings. And walking isn't going to take me far enough from this.

Chapter 3: The Visionary

Some people dream in images. I dream in metaphors.

I was the kid who thought words could save us. Who believed that if I spoke clearly enough, someone out there would feel less alone.

Now, I walk a barren sea of thought, carrying truths like offerings—treading lightly so I don't sink beneath the weight of everything I still believe.

Maybe I turned water into wine, but I never drank it. I gave everything away and forgot to hold some back for myself.

Still, I speak. Words are the only sword I know. Maybe they'll crucify me for it. Maybe I'll go unheard. But either way, I won't stop.

I was born to write what others are afraid to feel.

Chapter 4: Holding On

Some of us stay longer than we should. Not just in relationships, but in beliefs, in hopes, in places we no longer recognize.

I've been holding out for so long that I forgot what I was even waiting for. Hope burned at both ends, and the flame met in the middle, scorching everything it touched.

I've prayed. I've bargained. I've dreamed and then woken up mid-sentence. The nightmares flourish. The dreams remain still—stuck in the corners of my mind like photographs of people who've left.

I ask questions no one answers:
Do we keep waiting for a miracle, or is waiting the thing that's breaking us?

Sometimes I wonder, if I let go, would I fall? Or would I finally fly?

Chapter 5: What's the Easiest Way Out?

There are moments when two people know the truth, but both are too afraid to say it. So they part ways in silence, pretending not to notice the goodbye.

When she turned to leave, I didn't stop her. I just sat with the pieces of something that used to feel whole, trying to understand where I disappeared.

She had forgotten the promises. I had forgotten how to be seen.

After enough time, you start wearing masks so well that no one—not even you—can see beneath them.

And if they did? If they peeled back your flesh and looked beneath the performance?

Would they understand what you've become? Would they care?

Chapter 6: Flickers of Hope

There were days I believed in something better. When the air felt lighter, when the weight on my chest loosened just enough to let a full breath in.

I remember laughter—not always mine, but laughter all the same. The kind that lived between people and made things feel full, even if only for a moment.

I used to want to bottle it. Keep it in a jar like fireflies. Something to hold close on nights when the dark felt endless.

But hope isn't something you bottle. It flickers. It dims. Sometimes it goes out.

Still, for reasons I don't fully understand, I keep chasing it. Maybe we all do.

Chapter 7: The Fear of Knowing

There was a time when uncertainty terrified me. The not knowing, the what-ifs, the endless loops of imagined endings.

But lately, I've found something even heavier: the knowing.

The certainty of loss. The slow decay of something you once believed would last. The moment you realize that love doesn't always outlast time.

We all reach a point where we stop fearing the unknown because what's ahead is already written—and we're just walking toward it.

The clock is always moving. And whether we run or freeze, time doesn't care. It keeps going.

Chapter 8: Waiting Rooms and Goodbyes

Hospitals smell like sterilized endings. Like whispered prayers that go unanswered.

I've spent too much time in those rooms—where names are called, but not always returned. Where silence settles in like fog and time stretches between heartbeats.

It's a cruel thing, to watch monitors and measure life in numbers and beeping sounds. To wait for someone's last breath while pretending they still have more.

Not all goodbyes are spoken. Some are written in the hush of machines, in the slow slipping of a hand out of yours, in the way the world keeps turning even after the person you love stops.

Chapter 9: The Year Without Sun

There was a time when light meant something different. Not just survival. Not just proof that the earth kept turning.

I don't remember when I stopped noticing the sun. I just know there was a stretch of days— weeks, maybe months—where I was awake, but not alive.

I moved. I showed up. I functioned. But everything felt muted.

The world spun, but I felt left behind. Like the light forgot me. Or I forgot how to feel it.

And now, when it touches my skin again, it doesn't warm the same way. But I still turn my face toward it. Out of habit. Out of hope.

Chapter 10: Shadows of Yesterday

I walked through the neighborhood I grew up in. The buildings looked the same. The sidewalks still cracked in the places I used to trip.

But something had changed. Or maybe I had.

There's a strange feeling when you return to places that shaped you. It's like they remember a version of you that you no longer recognize.

I passed the house where I first fell in love. The fence we used to climb. The streetlight I stood under when I thought I had everything figured out.

Ghosts of who I was lingered everywhere—not to haunt, just to remind me:

You never really leave a place.
It just learns how to live without you.

Chapter 11: Small Miracles

Sometimes, it's not the big things that keep us going. It's the small ones—the unnoticed, almost accidental kindnesses the world throws our way.

A hand that reaches for yours when you didn't even realize you were drowning. A song that comes on the radio at just the right time, like someone—or something—knew what you needed.

The first breath of cool air after weeks of suffocating heat.

These aren't life-changing moments. But sometimes they're life-saving.

Most people don't even see them. But when you're close to the edge, you learn to pay attention to small miracles.

And sometimes, that's enough.

Chapter 12: What We Leave Behind

We all want to believe we'll be remembered. That something of us will echo after we're gone.

But the truth is, we're mostly just fragments. A collection of words—spoken and unspoken. Laughter that faded into walls. Touch that warmed for a moment, then vanished.

We build things. We say things. We love people. And eventually, we leave it all behind.

Sometimes I wonder if I'm writing a story anyone will want to read. If the things I build will last. If I will last.

We are all just stories in the end. And no one really gets to choose how theirs is told.

Chapter 13: The Things We Carry

We carry more than we realize.

It's in the tightness in our chest, the heaviness in our steps, the things we avoid talking about. It's in the quiet moments when everything feels louder than it should.

We carry our past in our bodies. Our regrets in the way we hesitate. The ghosts of everyone we've ever loved in the way we reach for someone new.

And sometimes, we carry things that were never even ours to begin with.

I've thought about what it would feel like to set it all down. To walk without the weight. But I don't know who I'd be without it.

Maybe that's the hardest part.

Chapter 14: When the Wind Changes

There's a moment before a storm—just before the sky breaks—when everything goes still.

The wind holds its breath. The world waits.

Change feels like that sometimes. A quiet tension in the air. A sense that something is coming, but you don't know what. Or whether you're ready.

I've felt it in relationships. In jobs. In myself. That subtle shift. That internal hush.

Sometimes change comes like thunder. Other times, it sneaks in on tiptoes.

But either way, the wind always changes.

And when it does, you either move with it or get left behind.

Chapter 15: The Longest Night

Some nights stretch forever.

The clock slows down. The dark thickens. Your thoughts become louder than anything outside your head.

I've had nights like that. Nights where you lie in bed and wonder if the sun forgot to rise. Where hope feels like a story someone told you a long time ago and you're not sure you believed it then either.

It's in those nights that you meet the deepest parts of yourself—the ones you hide during the day. The ones that only come out when the rest of the world is asleep.

But even the longest night ends. Eventually, something shifts. A new hour. A breath. A whisper of light.

And you remember that dawn doesn't ask for permission.
It just comes.

Chapter 16: Fear and Faith

Fear knows how to get comfortable. It moves in quietly and settles in your chest like it belongs there. It whispers every reason to stay still, to play it safe, to never try.

It's easy to listen to fear. It's loud. Familiar. It wears the mask of logic and calls itself protection.

Faith, though—that's different. Faith is quieter. More fragile. It's the soft voice inside that says maybe. Maybe it will work. Maybe it will get better. Maybe it's worth trying.

I've listened to fear long enough. Maybe now it's time to give faith a turn.

Chapter 17: The Art of Letting Go

Letting go doesn't happen all at once. It's not one decision, one tear, one goodbye.

It's a process. A thousand small releases. It's waking up and realizing something feels lighter. It's remembering without hurting.

Some things take longer to loosen their grip. Some memories hang on like vines.

But over time, fingers unclench. The ache softens. The space between you and what used to be grows wide enough to breathe.

And eventually, you realize you've let go.

Without even noticing, you've let go.

Chapter 18: The Places We Return To

We all have places we go back to. Sometimes it's a physical space. Sometimes, it's a memory. A conversation. A moment we didn't get to finish.

We return not because they were perfect, but because something there still feels unresolved.

Maybe we're looking for closure. Or maybe just proof that we've changed.

Sometimes we go back to see if what hurt still hurts.
And sometimes, we go back hoping it finally won't.

Chapter 19: Borrowed Time

Time isn't something we own. It's something we borrow. And we act like the loan is endless.

We spend it like it doesn't cost anything. Like there will always be more.

But time runs out. Sometimes suddenly. Sometimes slowly.

And the truth is, most of us don't spend it wisely.

We waste it on silence, on pride, on things that don't matter.

If I had more time, I'd like to think I'd use it better.

But I probably wouldn't.

Chapter 20: And Yet, We Begin Again

The world doesn't stop for our grief.

It keeps spinning. The sun keeps rising. The seasons change whether we're ready or not.

And so—somehow—we begin again.

Not because we're healed. Not because we're okay. But because there's nothing else to do.

Because hope is stubborn. Because love lingers. Because maybe, just maybe, the next beginning will be different.

And because the story isn't over yet.

Chapter 21: The Weight of Dreams

Dreams don't always inspire. Sometimes, they haunt.

Some dreams change over time, growing quieter, heavier. Others stay loud, even when we try to bury them.

There are dreams I've carried for years—some I still believe in, others I can barely recognize.

I don't know which ones I'll ever see through. But they all live inside me, pulling at me in different ways.

Even the ones I've let go of still leave shadows.

Chapter 22: The Echo of Footsteps

Sometimes, when the world goes still, I hear footsteps behind me. Not real ones. Echoes.

Memories of who I was. Of people I used to know.

We all carry the past. Sometimes it walks quietly beside us. Sometimes it catches up and taps us on the shoulder.

I don't mind the echoes anymore. They remind me how far I've come.

They remind me I'm still moving forward.

Chapter 23: A Window Left Open

Not everyone slams the door when they leave.

Some leave a window cracked.

Just enough to let the wind through. Just enough to make you wonder if they meant to close it all the way.

That almost-invitation. That silent question: Are you still there?

It's the hardest kind of goodbye. The kind that doesn't close.

And never fully lets you move on.

Chapter 24: The Roads We Take

We make choices every day—turn left, turn right, say yes, say nothing.

Some roads we choose. Others feel like they choose us.

And sometimes we look back and wonder—if we'd gone the other way, would we be happier? Would we be someone else entirely?

The truth is, we'll never know.

And maybe that's the price of moving forward.

Chapter 25: A Familiar Stranger

There was a time when I looked in the mirror and knew who I was.

Now, I see someone tired. Someone changed. Someone with memories I can't explain and emotions I haven't sorted out.

I hear my voice and sometimes it doesn't sound like mine.

It's strange—being familiar to everyone else, but feeling like a stranger to yourself.

Scott Burton

Part II: The Silence That Carries Memory

Some echoes don't fade. They just become part of the room.

Scott Burton

Chapter 26: The Kindness of Strangers

Sometimes it's not the people closest to you who show up when you need it most.

Sometimes it's a stranger—someone who doesn't owe you anything—who sees you.

A smile. A held door. A simple moment of understanding.

No big speech. No expectation. Just grace, quietly offered.

It reminds me that the world isn't always cruel. And that sometimes, the smallest kindness can undo the heaviest day.

Chapter 27: The Last Time We Spoke

It's strange what we remember.

I've replayed a hundred conversations between us, but I can't remember the last thing we said.

Was it something ordinary? A throwaway line? Something I didn't realize would be final?

Funny how the words that mattered most sometimes get lost.

And the ones that meant nothing echo the loudest.

Chapter 28: The Things That Stay

Most things fade.

Pain softens. Faces blur. Even the most vivid moments start to lose their edge with time.

But not everything disappears.

There are songs that anchor us to a season, a scent that transports us instantly to a memory we thought we'd forgotten. Some things—certain laughs, touches, voices—become part of the architecture of who we are. They remain when everything else has changed.

I don't cling to the past. But I live beside it. And it whispers in ways the present never will.

Chapter 29: The Morning After the Storm

There's a moment after every storm when everything is still.

The world holds its breath. The air smells clean. The ground is soaked, but quiet.

I've felt that moment in my chest—after the panic, after the spiral, after the breakdown.

It's not peace exactly. But it's something close.

It's the beginning of a rebuild.

Chapter 30: The Unfinished Sentence

Some words never find their ending.
Some thoughts stall in the middle, suspended
between fear and truth. I've held so many in my
mouth, waiting for the right moment to speak—
but it never came.

Maybe I was too afraid to be wrong. Or too
hopeful that silence could somehow be enough.

But unfinished sentences leave echoes. They
linger. They fill the room long after everyone has
gone, asking to be completed even when no one
is listening anymore.

Chapter 31: What Comes Next

I've spent so long looking back—replaying what was said, what wasn't, what I could have done differently. Memory became a ritual. Regret, a compass.

But the past offers no map for the future.

What comes next? I still don't know. But I'm learning that not knowing is its own kind of freedom. A blank page, terrifying and full of promise.

Maybe what comes next is less about the path and more about choosing to walk it.

Chapter 32: The Road Ahead

The road in front of me is unclear. It always has been.
Even when I thought I knew where I was going, I was mostly guessing. Trusting instinct. Following the pull of something I couldn't name.

And now, as I stand here again, trying to take the next step, I realize I've never really been lost. Just hesitant.

There's no map for becoming. Just movement.

Chapter 33: The Lives We Do Not Live

Every decision leaves behind a version of us.

Every yes is a thousand quiet no's. Every turn we take closes off another path.

Sometimes I think about who I might've been—if I'd said something else, chosen differently, loved someone longer.

Those lives don't haunt me.

But they do stay close.

Chapter 34: The Man at the Café

He stirred his coffee like he had nowhere to be.

Each motion slow. Deliberate. Like he was waiting for someone, or maybe remembering someone who wasn't coming.

I watched him through the glass and wondered if that's what acceptance looked like—stillness, not sadness.

Maybe he wasn't lost. Maybe he had just stopped trying to arrive.

Chapter 35: The Sound of Empty Streets

Midnight is when the world exhales.

No footsteps. No voices. Just the hum of streetlights blinking into nothingness. It's a kind of silence that demands attention—not because it's loud, but because it makes everything else feel louder.

In these empty moments, I hear myself clearly. The doubts, the grief, the questions I push aside during the day come forward like old friends asking to be seen.

And maybe that's why I love empty streets. They don't pretend. They just wait.

Chapter 36: The Distance Between Knowing and Becoming

There's a difference between knowing and becoming.

You can understand your pain and still repeat it. You can name the pattern and still walk the same path. Awareness feels like progress—but it's only the beginning.

Becoming is harder. It's action without applause. Change without clarity. It's choosing differently even when the old habits still whisper comfort.

Most of us live somewhere in between—aware of who we were, unsure of who we're becoming.

But we move anyway.
And maybe that's enough.

Chapter 37: The Weight of an Apology

"I'm sorry" doesn't always come out in words.

Sometimes it lives in the pause. The way someone avoids your eyes. The way they say everything except what they should.

And sometimes, we carry apologies no one is ever going to hear.

Because saying it out loud doesn't always fix what's already broken.

But silence doesn't heal it either.

Chapter 38: The Shape of Fear

Fear isn't always dramatic.

Sometimes it's subtle. A pause before you answer. A decision you keep postponing. A truth you refuse to say out loud.

It wears different masks—fear of failure, fear of loss, fear of being known too well.

It shapes how we live, even when we pretend we're not afraid.

The hardest part is realizing how much it's already taken.

Chapter 39: Love and Other Illusions

We talk about love like it's simple. But it's not.

It changes shape depending on where you stand. Up close, it's messy. From a distance, it looks perfect.

Maybe I've loved illusions more than people. Maybe I've been in love with the idea of being loved.

Either way, love was never the problem.

The stories we told ourselves about it were.

Chapter 40: The Spaces Between Us

There's a distance that wasn't always there.

It grew slowly—between conversations, missed calls, unanswered texts. Between all the things we didn't say.

I used to try to bridge it. Now I just stare at it, wondering when the space between us became the whole story.

And whether it's still mine to close.

Chapter 41: The Sound of Rain

Rain has always been a kind of comfort to me.

The way it blankets the silence, drowns out the noise of everything else, and makes the world feel smaller, more manageable.

I stand in it sometimes, just to feel something. Letting it soak through my clothes, my skin, all the way to where I've gone numb.

There's something about storms—how they arrive loud, then leave the world feeling cleaner.

Sometimes, I think I'm waiting for one of those storms to pass through me.

Chapter 42: The Art of Beginning Again

We start over more than we admit.

After loss. After failure. After someone leaves. After we leave ourselves.

Beginning again doesn't mean pretending the past didn't happen. It means carrying it forward in a way that doesn't crush us.

It's hard. It's slow. It's necessary.

And even if you've done it a dozen times, the next one still feels like the first.

Chapter 43: The Ghosts We Carry

Not all ghosts are dead.

Some are memories of people we once were.
Versions of ourselves we can't quite return to.
Relationships that ended without clarity.

I carry mine quietly.

They don't scream or haunt. They just linger—in
habits, in hesitations, in the way I love now.

They don't want to be forgotten.
Only remembered with honesty.

Chapter 44: The Weight of Waiting

Waiting is a kind of invisible heaviness.

It doesn't show on your face, but you feel it in your steps, in your breath, in your inability to rest.

Waiting for change. For clarity. For someone to reach out. For something to finally feel different.

It wears you down in ways even grief can't.

Because at least grief has a name.
Waiting just leaves you in limbo.

Chapter 45: The Moments We Never Knew Were Lasts

You rarely recognize a last moment when it happens.

The last hug. The last "I love you." The last time their name lit up your phone.

We think we'll get a warning. But most endings don't come with announcements.

They slip by unnoticed. And it's only later—days, months, years—that we look back and realize:

That was it.
That was the last time.

Chapter 46: The Echo of a Name

Some names still feel like home. Even when the person behind them is long gone.

I avoid saying your name out loud, not because I've forgotten, but because I haven't.

It still tastes like a memory I'm not ready to let dissolve.

Some names are keys. Some are locks.
Yours is both.

Chapter 47: The Weight of an Unfinished Story

Not all stories get endings.

Some just stop. A sentence mid-thought. A silence that was never broken. A goodbye that never came.

We carry them—these half-written moments—as if one day we might pick up the thread and continue.

But some stories were only meant to teach us something in their incompleteness.

Maybe this one was, too.

Chapter 48: Learning to Love the Quiet

For a long time, I filled the silence with noise.

Music. Talking. Thoughts I didn't want to face.

But silence isn't the enemy. It's where the real things rise to the surface. It's where truths sit, waiting to be heard.

I'm learning not to run from the quiet.

Sometimes, it says more than words ever could.

Chapter 49: The Roads That Lead Home

Home isn't always a house.

Sometimes it's a person. A smell. A moment you keep returning to in your mind.

I've taken roads that led me far from what felt familiar. Some of those roads taught me who I was. Others taught me what I never want again.

Maybe home isn't something you find.
Maybe it's something you create—step by step, day by day.

Chapter 50: The Space Between Heartbeats

There's a pause between heartbeats. Between inhale and exhale. Between the thought and the word.

That space is where we live most of our lives— between what was and what will be.

It's easy to miss it. But I think that's where the real moments hide.

The stillness.
The choices.
The truth.

Scott Burton

Part III: The Weather Inside Us

You can survive the storm and still not know how to live in the sun.

Scott Burton

Chapter 51: The People Who Leave and the People Who Stay

Some people leave like a slammed door—sudden and loud. Others drift away like smoke, fading so slowly you don't realize they're gone until they are.

But some stay. Through the mess. Through the silence. Through the ache.

Hold onto those people. They are rare.

Not everyone will stand beside you when you don't have anything to offer but the weight of your own heart.

Chapter 52: The Unspoken Goodbyes

Not all goodbyes are said out loud.

Some are felt in the way someone pulls away. In how they stop asking. In how they go quiet without explanation.

I used to wait for the words. Now I know better.

Absence can speak louder than anything.
And some goodbyes happen in silence.

Chapter 53: The Art of Moving On

Moving on isn't a moment. It's not a clean break or a perfect line in the sand.

It's waking up and realizing you're not waiting anymore. It's remembering without aching.

It's the slow loosening of the past's grip.

And when it happens—really happens—it doesn't feel like forgetting.

It feels like breathing.

Chapter 54: The Sound of Footsteps at Midnight

There's something sacred about the world at midnight.

Empty streets. Long shadows. The soft hum of streetlights buzzing above silence.

It's where overthinkers go to walk off memories. Where hearts whisper the things they're not brave enough to say at noon.

I've walked those streets. Maybe you have too.

It's quiet out there. But never truly empty.

Chapter 55: The Places We Can Never Return To

You can go back to the same street, the same house, the same coffee shop.

But it won't be the same. You won't be the same.

Time rewrites everything, quietly.

We don't notice until we're standing there, realizing the ghosts are gone or we've become one of them.

Some places let us visit.
But never let us belong again.

Chapter 56: The Moon Knows Our Secrets

The moon has watched every version of me. Every quiet night. Every whispered wish. Every I miss you I didn't say.

It's seen all of us, really.

That's the thing about the moon—it reflects light, but it carries darkness too.

And when I look up at it, I wonder if it remembers all the versions of me that no one else ever met.

Chapter 57: The Weight of Forgiveness

Forgiveness isn't about pretending something didn't happen. It's not letting someone off the hook.

It's setting yourself free from bitterness.

I used to think forgiving meant saying, "It's okay." Now I know it means saying, "I'm done carrying this."

Sometimes we forgive to heal someone else.

But mostly, we forgive so we can finally rest.

Chapter 58: The Quiet After the Storm

There's a hush after the worst has passed.

It's not peace. Not yet. But it's the beginning of it.

The air feels different. The light returns, slowly.

I've felt it in myself—after the fight, after the breakdown, after the grief. That pause. That breath.

It doesn't mean the storm didn't do damage. It means you're still standing.

Chapter 59: The End and the Beginning

Every ending is a doorway.
Even the ones we didn't choose. Even the ones that come with silence instead of closure.

Grief disguises itself as finality. But sometimes, the deepest losses teach us how to begin again.

Not because we're ready. Not because we've healed. But because life insists. Because the heart continues its quiet rhythm, even after being broken.

Chapter 60: The Final Whisper

If I could leave you with one thing, it would be this:

You are not what you've lost.
Not what you've endured.
Not the people who left or the things that broke.

You're still here.

And as long as you're still here, there's more to feel. More to give. More to become.

The story isn't over.
Not yet.

Chapter 61: The Sound of an Empty House

An empty house has a weight to it.

The floors creak louder. The silence stretches wider.

It's not just the absence of noise—it's the memory of it. The echoes of laughter that once filled the rooms. The conversations that used to bounce off the walls.

I've walked through quiet rooms and felt them hum with what used to be.

And sometimes, I wonder if they miss us too.

Chapter 62: The Shape of a Scar

Scars don't form overnight.

They build over time—layer by layer, pain by pain, until healing starts.

Some close cleanly. Others leave marks you can't hide.

I have both. The visible and the invisible.

And while I don't wear them proudly, I no longer hide them either.

They remind me I survived.

Chapter 63: The Weight of Old Photographs

I found an old photograph today.

It was just a moment. Smiles frozen in time. People who don't look like that anymore. People I don't talk to anymore.

But holding it was like holding the past in my hand.

Light, but heavy.
Distant, but personal.

Strange how much one image can carry.

Chapter 64: The Distance Between Then and Now

There was a time when I thought I knew exactly where I was going.

Everything felt mapped. Clear. Linear.

But now, the path is blurry. The signs faded. The certainty gone.

And maybe that's okay. Maybe certainty was never the goal.

Maybe life is more about finding ourselves in the detours.

Chapter 65: The Way We Say I Love You

Not all love is spoken.

Sometimes it's the way we remember their coffee order, the way we stay when they're quiet, the way we give space when space is needed—even if it hurts.

We say "I love you" in glances, in gestures, in the silences we don't rush to fill.

Love is not always loud. But it's always present— if you're listening.

Chapter 66: The Gravity of Small Moments

I used to think life was built from milestones. Big days. Loud events. Announcements.

But the more I live, the more I realize life happens in the quiet places.

The way someone touches your shoulder when you need grounding. The extra blanket folded on the edge of the bed. The silence that feels safe, not empty.

We overlook the small moments, but they're the ones that shape us.

They're the ones that stay.

Chapter 67: The Storms We Carry

There are storms we walk through. And then there are storms we carry inside.

The ones that don't pass. The ones that rumble beneath our skin, waiting.

Some leave damage. Others leave clarity. Most leave both.

I'm still learning what mine has left behind. But I know it changed me.

Chapter 68: The Doors We Never Open

Some doors stay shut, not because we don't have the key—
but because we already know what's on the other side.

There are letters I'll never send. Conversations I'll never start. Feelings I'll never confess.

It's not fear. It's acceptance.

Some things are meant to remain unspoken.
And maybe that's okay.

Chapter 69: The Things We Were Supposed to Be

I've thought a lot about the versions of me that never existed.

The ones who said yes instead of no. Who stayed. Who left. Who tried again.

In another life, maybe I'm someone else entirely. Or maybe I'm still wondering the same things.

Either way, it reminds me—
We can only live one life at a time.

Chapter 70: The Quiet Between Heartbeats

There's a space between heartbeats. Between breaths. Between thoughts.
A stillness that most people miss.

But in that stillness, I find something honest. A truth that doesn't need to be spoken. A presence that doesn't need to be proven.

Maybe that's where peace lives—not in the doing, but in the space between.

Chapter 71: The Weight of a Name

Some names carry more than identity.

They hold memories. Histories. Emotions too big to speak.

When you said my name, it felt like something more. Like home. Like truth. Like a version of me I liked better.

Now, I hear it from strangers, and it sounds empty.

Because the weight wasn't in the name.
It was in the way you said it.

Chapter 72: The Roads That Lead Nowhere

We've all taken roads that led to dead ends. Chased promises that vanished. Built futures on foundations that cracked the moment we stepped forward.

But those roads weren't wasted. They taught us. Broke us. Showed us what we would and wouldn't do again.

The roads that lead nowhere still move us. And sometimes, that's enough.

Chapter 73: The Things We Learn Too Late

Some lessons don't come in time.

You learn them only after the moment has passed, the damage is done, the person is gone.

I've found the right words only after they were no longer needed.

If I could go back, I'd say more. I'd stay longer. I'd listen better.

But time doesn't rewind.
It only reflects.

Chapter 74: The Ghosts of What Could Have Been

Not all ghosts haunt houses.
Some haunt hearts.

The versions of ourselves we never became. The love we didn't reach for. The words we rehearsed but never spoke.

They linger in our quiet moments. In the pause before sleep. In the shadow of a thought we can't quite place.

We don't need to be haunted forever.
But we do have to look them in the eye.

Chapter 75: The Softness of a Morning Alone

Some mornings arrive quietly. They don't ask anything of you.

No plans. No deadlines. Just sunlight filtering through the blinds and the gentle weight of your own thoughts.

There's something healing in that. In not rushing. In simply being.
I sip my coffee slower on those days, let the stillness wrap around me like a blanket I didn't know I needed.

And for once, I don't feel behind.

Scott Burton

Part IV: The Pulse That Keeps Going

Not every heartbeat wants to be heard.
Some just want to keep going.

Scott Burton

Chapter 76: The Weight of Almost

Almost is a heavy word.
It carries every version of us that nearly was.
Every chance we didn't take. Every love that
nearly bloomed but never took root.

There's a grief in the almost. A quiet ache.
Because we saw the shape of something
beautiful—we just couldn't reach it.

And maybe that's what makes almost harder than
never.

Chapter 77: The Sound of a Fading Echo

There was a time your voice lived everywhere. In songs I couldn't stop playing. In the corners of rooms we once stood in. In the quiet hum of my own thoughts.

Now it's a whisper I barely hear. Still there, but thinner. Like a thread pulled too far.

Sometimes I want to pull it back. But echoes aren't meant to last forever.

Chapter 78: The Things That Make Us Stay

We stay for different reasons.
Sometimes it's love. Sometimes it's guilt.
Often, it's the weight of memory—thick with the promise that things could be like they once were.

But staying isn't always a virtue.
It's a decision. And sometimes it keeps us from the things we truly need.

Knowing the difference is the hard part.

Chapter 79: The Space Between Goodbye and Forgetting

Goodbye is never the end.
It's just the moment we stop pretending that everything will stay the same.

For a while, there's a space—where memories still visit, where voices still linger. We remember the good and bad in uneven waves.

Then, slowly, forgetting creeps in. Not out of malice.
But because life makes room for what's next.

Chapter 80: The Story That Still Isn't Over

Some stories don't have neat endings.
They stop mid-sentence. Fade to silence. Get interrupted by life, time, distance.

But unfinished doesn't mean untrue.

The words still live in us. Waiting.
And maybe one day we'll pick up the thread again and write the rest.

Until then, the story continues—just differently.

Chapter 81: The Silence Between Us

There was a time when our silence felt safe.
It meant comfort, understanding. We didn't need
to fill the space with noise to know we were still
close.

But now it's something else.
A distance. A boundary neither of us wants to
acknowledge, but both of us feel.

Silence still speaks.
I just wish I knew what it was saying.

Chapter 82: The Weight of Promises

Promises aren't always loud.
Some are whispered in quiet moments, never meant to be broken. Others are made to ourselves, scribbled in thought, never spoken aloud.

But when they break—no matter how softly— they leave a sound that lingers.

It's not always about betrayal.
Sometimes it's just the ache of something unfinished.

Chapter 83: The Moon and Me

I look up at the moon and it feels familiar.
Constant. Distant. Always watching.

There are nights it feels like the only one who's
seen every version of me. The one who knows the
thoughts I don't speak and the prayers I don't say
out loud.

We don't talk, the moon and I.
But sometimes, I feel like it understands.

Chapter 84: The Places We Leave Pieces of Ourselves

We don't just pass through places—we leave parts of ourselves behind.

A laugh caught on a summer breeze.
A heartbreak echoing in the walls of a room.
A version of ourselves sitting on a park bench, still waiting for closure.

I walk by those places and feel something shift.
Like a ghost brushing past.

Not everything leaves when we do.

Chapter 85: The Art of Disappearing

There are different ways to disappear.

Some people leave all at once—a slammed door,
an empty room, a silence too sharp to ignore.
Others fade slowly. A text unanswered. A visit
delayed. A version of themselves that stops
showing up.

I've been both.
The one who vanished and the one left blinking at
the space where someone used to be.

And sometimes, we disappear from ourselves
long before anyone notices.

Chapter 86: The Weight of What If

"What if" is a shadow that follows even when you stop looking back.

What if I had stayed?
What if I had spoken up?
What if I had walked away sooner?

The questions don't go away. They evolve.
They grow quieter, but never leave.

I've come to realize that regret isn't always about mistakes.
It's about the chances we never gave ourselves.

Chapter 87: The Things That Wake Us in the Night

There's a moment in the middle of the night where everything feels louder.

The creak of the floor. The hum of your thoughts. The weight of memories that waited all day for the dark.

Sometimes it's a dream. Sometimes it's a name. Other times, it's just silence that feels like it's holding its breath.

And there you are, wide awake, wondering if this is when the truth comes knocking.

Chapter 88: The Sound of a Closing Door

Some doors close with finality. Others barely make a sound.

But either way, you know when something's over.
You feel the shift.
The room feels colder. The air tighter. The echo a little too long.

I've stood on both sides.
Leaving. Being left.
Both come with questions that never really get answered.

Chapter 89: The Fragility of Happiness

Happiness is softer than we admit.
Not loud, not permanent—just something that
arrives quietly and leaves the same way.

I've chased it.
Held it too tightly and watched it slip through my
fingers.
Ignored it, and didn't realize it was there until it
was gone.

It's not meant to be caged.
It's meant to be noticed while it's here.

Chapter 90: The Things We Try to Forget

We all have things we don't want to remember.

Words we wish we never said.
Moments we wish we'd handled differently.
People who saw the worst in us—or brought it out.

But forgetting isn't clean.
It leaves smudges.
And memory has a way of returning when you least expect it—wearing new faces, saying old names.

Chapter 91: The Weight of a Single Moment

One moment can split a life in two.

A look.
A word.
A decision made too quickly—or not quickly enough.

We don't always see the pivot until it's behind us. But looking back, we can trace everything to that one breath where everything changed.

And wonder who we'd be if we'd just blinked a second later.

Chapter 92: The Quiet Side of Love

Love isn't always loud.

Sometimes it's in the way someone stays.
The way they remember your coffee order.
The way they don't interrupt your silence.

We're taught to look for grand gestures.
But it's the quiet ones that last.

The kind that doesn't ask to be seen—just hopes to be felt.

Chapter 93: The Roads We Take Alone

There are journeys no one can take with you.

Even the ones who love you can only walk beside
you so far.
At some point, you step into a stretch of road that
is yours alone.

That's where the hard questions live.
Who am I without them?
Where does this path lead?

It's lonely.
But it's also where truth begins to speak.

Chapter 94: The Gravity of an Empty Room

An empty room can feel heavier than a crowded one.

Not because of what's there—but because of what isn't.
No laughter. No voices. No signs that someone once lived in it.

But the silence carries memories.
They cling to corners and echoes and the spots where sunlight hits just right.

You can almost hear what used to be said there.

Almost.

Chapter 95: The Stories We Tell Ourselves

We all build narratives.

To explain who we are. Why we left. Why we stayed.

Some stories keep us safe.
Others keep us stuck.

I'm trying to tell a new one.
One where I'm not always the one who's hurting.

Chapter 96: The Weight of an Unfinished Sentence

Not everything gets to be completed.

Some apologies never come. Some truths never get voiced. Some feelings stay just below the surface.

I've learned to live with ellipses.
To accept that some things remain open.

Chapter 97: The Places Where Time Stands Still

There are places where time doesn't move.

An old bedroom. A familiar street. A voicemail you haven't deleted.

They don't change.
You do.

And that's what makes it hard.

Chapter 98: The Things We Carry Forward

We don't leave everything behind.

Some things come with us—lessons, scars, memories, dreams.

We get to choose what we carry.
And who we become because of it.

Chapter 99: The End of the Road

Every road ends eventually.

But endings aren't the same as conclusions.

Sometimes the road stops, and we find another.

Sometimes the stop is what saves us.

Chapter 100: The Story That Never Truly Ends

Maybe there is no final chapter.

Maybe stories go on in the people we become, the ones we love, the things we create.

I don't know how this one ends.

But I do know this:
As long as you're still here,
there's still more to write.

Scott Burton

About the Author

Scott Burton is a writer, poet, and emotional archivist. His work blends lyrical prose with raw honesty, exploring themes of grief, longing, resilience, and the ongoing search for meaning. He writes from lived experience—often shaped by illness, recovery, distance, and the deep ache of love lost or never fully reached.

As the author of *Chaos: A Journal of Being Human*, Burton invites readers into the quiet emotional spaces we often carry alone—the ache we don't name, the truths we avoid, the beauty buried inside what breaks us. His style flows between poetry and prose, guided more by feeling than form, offering words for the things we struggle to say out loud.

His earlier writing took shape in hospital rooms, late-night notes, and unfinished messages that found their way into these pages. Future collections will continue to explore that space between silence and survival, where memory meets vulnerability and the human spirit persists.

He lives in North Carolina, where he continues to write in the in-between hours—crafting pages that remember, reach, and begin again.

www.ingramcontent.com/pod-product-compliance
Lightning Source LLC
Chambersburg PA
CBHW071523120626
46550CB00006B/2341